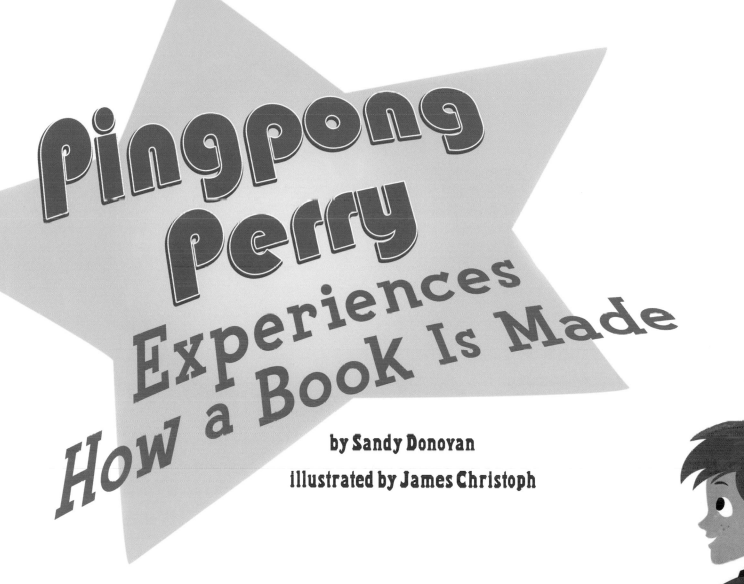

Pingpong Perry

Experiences How a Book Is Made

by Sandy Donovan

illustrated by James Christoph

PICTURE WINDOW BOOKS
a capstone imprint

Thanks to our advisers for their expertise, research, and advice:

Diane R. Chen, Library Information Specialist
John F. Kennedy Middle School
Nashville, Tennessee

Terry Flaherty, Ph.D, Professor of English
Minnesota State University, Mankato

Editors: Shelly Lyons and Jennifer Besel
Designer: Abbey Fitzgerald
Art Director: Nathan Gassman
Production Specialist: Jane Klenk
The illustrations in this book were created digitally.

Photo Credits: Capstone Studio/Karon Dubke, all

Picture Window Books
151 Good Counsel Drive
P.O. Box 669
Mankato, MN 56002-0669
877-845-8392
www.capstonepub.com

Library of Congress Cataloging-in-Publication Data
Donovan, Sandra, 1967-
Pingpong Perry experiences how a book is made / by Sandy
Donovan ; illustrated by James Christoph.
p. cm. — (In the library)
Includes index.
ISBN 978-1-4048-5759-9 (library binding)
ISBN 978-1-4048-6106-0 (paperback)
1. Books—Juvenile literature. 2. Publishers and publishing—
Juvenile literature. I. Christoph, James, ill. II. Title.
Z116.A2D66 2010
002—dc22
2009030400

Printed in the United States of America in North Mankato, Minnesota.
102010   005971R

This is Perry. Perry has a bike and a few freckles.

Perry likes pizza and pingpong more than anything else.
He especially likes pondering pizza while playing pingpong.

Perry is a published author. See his book? It's called *Perry's Practical Guide to the Pizza Picks of Popular Pingpong Players*. Isn't it great?

This is the story of how Perry's book was made.

3

It started like this.

Perry was playing pingpong. He was practicing the back door banana-curve serve. It's a sweet move. He learned it watching popular pingpong players.

He was also pondering pizza. Just then, Perry wondered what kind of pizza popular pingpong players pick.

All books begin as an idea. Perhaps a picture sparks an idea. A friend's remark can also lead to an idea. Most often, an author gets ideas from everyday life.

Perry rode his bike to the library. He looked in books. He checked out some Web sites. But he didn't find anything about the pizza picks of popular pingpong players.

The librarian helped him. But she found nothing. Finally she said,

"I don't know. I guess no one has written about that yet."

sorry there are no results for your search

ALMANAC

Perry was puzzled.

Then he had an idea.

He would find the answers. Then he would put the answers in a book.

First Perry read articles about popular pingpong players. But the articles didn't say anything about pizza.

HISTORY
of
PING

RULES

PINGPONG
CHAMP

Next he e-mailed some pingpong players. Most of them e-mailed back. They were happy to be in a book. They told Perry their pizza picks. One player even taught Perry a secret move. It was the hop-and-drop handcuff serve.

Dear Perry,

I would love to be in your book. I prefer my pizza Hawaiian style, topped with pineapple and ham.

Attached you will see my secret hop-and-drop handcuff serve.

Good luck!
–Karl

When an author collects information for his or her book, it's important to make sure the information is correct and current.

Finally Perry had all the information he needed. He began to write.

Perry sent his finished manuscript to a book publishing company.

Dear Publisher,

I have sent you my awesome book. It's about the pizza picks of popular pingpong players. I think you will agree, it's pretty powerful. Want to publish it?

Sincerely,

Perry

An author sends the manuscript to publishers. Often the author sends it to many publishers before it is accepted. Publishers are very picky about the books they choose. Making a book is expensive.

The publisher said, "No thanks."

Perry tried other publishers, too. Forty-one of them said, "No thanks." But the 42nd publisher pleasantly approved.

YES!

I ♥ PINGPONG

"The pizza picks of pingpong players?" she said. "Perfect!"

At the publishing company, an editor got Perry's manuscript. Her name was Tracy. She had some ideas to make the manuscript even better.

"Let's add what kind of paddles each player likes to use," Tracy said to Perry.

An editor works closely with the author. Together they work on the words until the sentences sound just right. An editor also makes sure the words match the pictures chosen for the book.

Tracy also helped improve the writing. She moved some words. She fixed spelling and punctuation. She sent the manuscript to a pingpong expert and checked all the facts. She also sent it to another editor for advice.

Peter Payton ~~preferrs~~ prefers pepperoni pizza from ~~a place called pizza plaza~~ Pizza Plaza. Peter's favorite ~~swerve~~ serve is the smash-and-dash delight. His most prized possession is his pingpong paddle named Penny.

A designer also got Perry's book. His name was Jason.
Tracy told Jason what she thought the book should look like.

Jason read the manuscript.
He had some ideas, too.

A designer talks to lots of people before creating a book's design, or appearance. Designers make the book exciting to look at. They also place the words on the page so they are easy to read.

Finally, Tracy and Jason chose the size and shape of Perry's book. They decided the cover should have a picture showing a pingpong paddle and pizza. They even talked about what the pages would look like.

Then Jason got to work designing the book on a computer.

PING PONG IDEAS

Perry's book needed pictures of popular pingpong players. It also needed pictures of pizza and pingpong paddles.

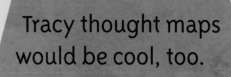

Tracy thought maps would be cool, too.

Maps would help readers see where the players lived.

Jason found a company that sold photographs of pingpong players. He bought the perfect pictures for the book. He also found a photographer to shoot photos of pizza and pingpong paddles.

Then he found an illustrator to draw the maps.

If a book will have photos, illustrations, or both, artists may need to be hired. Artists need plenty of time to draw the illustrations or shoot the pictures.

Jason put together each page of the book on his computer.

Tracy and Jason carefully checked the pages many times to make sure the words and pictures looked right.

Finally, the book was ready to be printed.

It was saved as a computer file. Then the file was sent to a book printing company. The printing company used the file and programed a giant printing press. The press printed out the book in huge sheets.

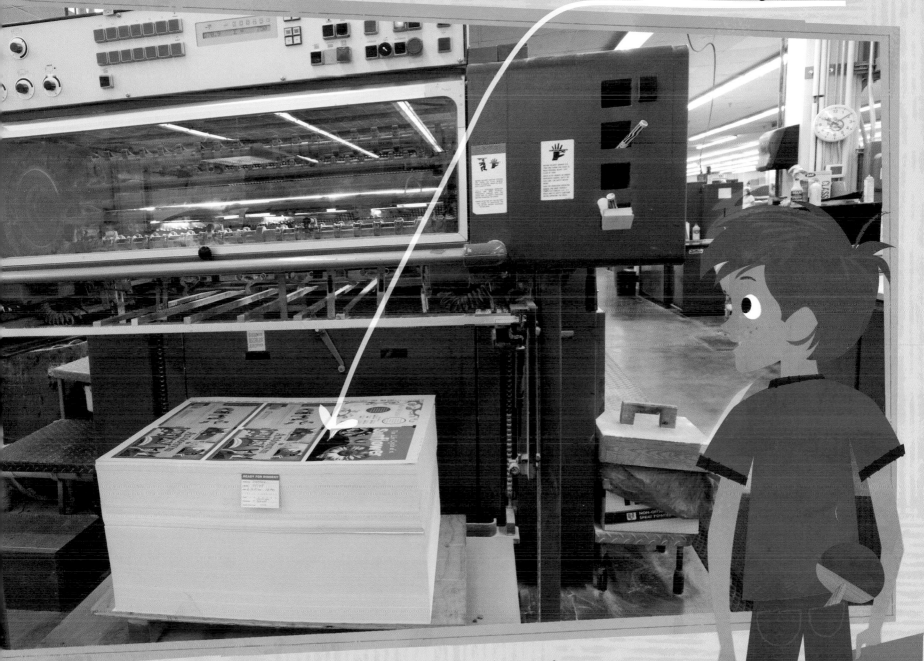

The huge sheets were cut into pages. The pages were glued together. Then a cover was added.

Members of the publisher's marketing team worked hard to sell the book. They talked about it with people at bookstores and libraries.

They wrote to magazines and newspapers.

PERR
PRACTICA

to the
Pizza Picks

P

PERRY'S
PRACTICAL GUIDE
to the
Pizza Picks
of Popular
Pingpong Players

They wrote to people at Web sites and other publications, too.

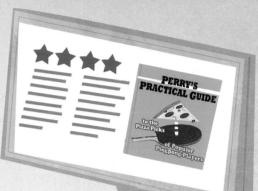

PERRY'S PRACTICAL GUIDE
to the Pizza Picks
of Popular Pingpong Players

Y'S GUIDE

of Popular ngpong Players

These publications wrote articles about the book. Their readers learned about it.

And soon everyone wanted to buy it.

Meet PERRY

Editing, designing, and printing a book are only part of a publisher's job. Publishers also work hard to sell the book. Authors help with this job, too.

At last everyone was able to find out about the pizza picks of popular pingpong players. Hurray! Perry threw a pizza party with peanuts, pop, and—of course—pizza. They played pingpong. Everyone had a great time.

But wait. Perry is already thinking about his next book. What will the title be?

It will be
The Cheese Choices of Chinese Checkers Champs.

Good luck, Perry!

22

Glossary

designer—a person who creates the way a book will look; designers use computer software to make designs.

editor—a person who works with an author to make the contents of a book as strong as possible; editors are responsible for making sure books are ready to be published.

illustrator—a person who draws pictures for a book; illustrators might draw by hand or on a computer.

manuscript—the text of the book that comes from the author

photographer—a person who takes pictures for a living

publications—books, magazines, journals, and other printed materials that are sold to the public

publisher—a company that makes books so people can buy them; the term *publisher* can also mean the person at a publishing company who is in charge of all books the company publishes.

More Books to Read

Carle, Eric. *Artist to Artist: 23 Major Illustrators Talk to Children About Their Art.* New York: Philomel Books, 2007.

Royston, Angela. *How Is a Book Made?* Chicago: Heinemann Library, 2005.

Schotter, Roni. *The Boy Who Loved Words.* New York: Schwartz & Wade Books, 2006.

Snyder, Inez. *Trees to Paper.* New York: Children's Press, 2003.

Internet Sites

FactHound offers a safe, fun way to find Internet sites related to this book. All of the sites on FactHound have been researched by our staff.

Here's all you do:

Visit *www.facthound.com*

FactHound will fetch the best sites for you!

Look for all the books in the
In the Library series:

- Bob the Alien Discovers the Dewey Decimal System
- Bored Bella Learns About Fiction and Nonfiction
- Karl and Carolina Uncover the Parts of a Book
- Pingpong Perry Experiences How a Book Is Made

Index